Stonework of the Sky

Stonework of the Sky

POETRY BY

Joseph A. Enzweiler

GRAYWOLF PRESS

Copyright 1994 by Joseph A. Enzweiler

Publication of this volume is made possible in part by a grant provided by the Minnesota State Arts Board through an appropriation by the Minnesota State Legislature, and by a grant from the National Endowment for the Arts. Significant additional support has been provided by the Andrew W. Mellon Foundation, the Lila Wallace – Reader's Digest Fund, the McKnight Foundation, and other generous contributions from foundations, corporations, and individuals. Graywolf Press is a member agency of United Arts, Saint Paul. To these organizations and individuals who make our work possible, we offer heartfelt thanks.

Published by GRAYWOLF PRESS
2402 University Avenue, Suite 203
Saint Paul, Minnesota 55114
All rights reserved. Printed in the United States of America.

9 8 7 6 5 4 3 2
First Graywolf Printing, 1994

Library of Congress Catalog Card Number 94-73113
ISBN 1-55597-222-5

For my family and my friends
who gave me their stories
that I could give them back again

and for Hannah, in a great room
dreaming

Contents

Foreword   3

The Flawed Stone and Hammer of Living Memory
Coming In   7
Honey Locust   8
Beyond   9
Stonework   10
Scything   12
The Great Stone Wall of Camp Springs, Kentucky   13
Sycamore   15
The Necessary Stranger   17
Flathead Six   18
Wild Basil   21

You Were Only Dream and I a Great Room Dreaming You
Dragonfly   25
The Rose   27
Wooden Carving   29
Starlight   30
The Heart   31
Spring   32
Summer   33
Autumn   34
Winter   35
Hannah   36
Tomorrow   37

A Creature Whose Brilliant Eyes You Missed for All Time
Sonnet for Woodstove   41
Porch in Winter   42
Old Black Dodge   43
The Burden   45
All of Those Cigars   47

The Lost	49
Jason	50
Douglas	51
Bob Gunn	52
Woman with a Damaged Leg	53

Of the Hunt, of Love, of Their Beautiful Defeat

The Man Who Stood Still	57
Love Poem for Bluebells	59
There Is Death I Said, Etc.	60
Sky, the Road, a Fire Between	62
Sonnet for Unknown Child	63
Sea of Storms	64
Antonín Becvár's Atlas	65
Boxcar	66
Dinner with Jack Palance	67
The Doorway	69

Stonework of the Sky

Foreword

During a panel discussion on poetry at the University of Alaska a few years ago, a local verse-maker remarked that the "university-trained poet" had in recent times become the accepted model; a fact that few would dispute. The question as to whether this was in all ways a good thing for poetry was not raised, and I will not attempt an answer here. The thought, however, does serve to remind us that there exists here and there, even now, another poetry, independent of academic rank and preference, and of a continuity with an older tradition represented by poets as different as John Clare, Thomas Hardy, and Edward Thomas.

The poems of Joseph Enzweiler seem to me in some way to belong to that older tradition, as well as to the more modern one most of us share. His first book, *Home Country,* appeared in a limited edition in 1986. Other than for a brief local notice, it received little attention and none outside Alaska; yet it was perhaps the finest volume of poetry to appear in the state for many years. Within its fifty-eight pages, with each of its three sections introduced by one of the author's photographs of the local woodland, the range of the poems was impressive.

Home Country gave the impression of being centered on Alaska, on the countryside Enzweiler knows well and where he has built a home. The poems celebrate, among other things, the winter season, the snowy night, the welcome to be found within the fire-warmed cabin, and do so with a quiet authority. This new collection has, it seems to me, less to do with Alaska, but is instead concentrated on that other home so many of us have come from, in his case Ohio and Kentucky; but also that greater home, Earth, and the starry space that surrounds and contains it.

In both *Home Country* and this new book the emotion that dominates the poem is love – love for the places where he has lived, in which he grew up, for the people who still live there, and for the work he has done, whether scything a field or building a stone wall. This devotion to a local human economy sets these poems apart from the bulk of contemporary poetry with its obsessive self-concern and incapacity for affection.

In their honesty of feeling, in their affection for a place and its people, the poems remind me at times of the few and genuine poems of Fred Bigjim, another poet of Alaska who remains unknown and unremarked on. They remind me also of painter Marsden Hartley, whose characteristic poems were nourished by his familiarity with and deep love for the Maine seacoast: its woods, waters and creatures. I think too that Edwin Muir might have liked these poems because of his enduring regard for the traditional habits of the countryman.

Good company for any poet, I would say. I admire the independence of these poems and the independence of their author. The poems are honest in their feeling and honest in their craft, in their use of the forms of verse. In their quiet attention to the details of our common life, they offer a moral lesson and a modest rebuke to the excesses of much contemporary poetry. I recommend them to the reader.

JOHN HAINES
1 JULY 1993

THE FLAWED STONE AND HAMMER OF LIVING MEMORY

Coming In

I hear them coming in from the field,
down the hillside, wind
lashing the fresh grass.
They are bringing the goats
in for the night.
He holds his Amish hat in place,
her dress blows sideways.
Squeal of a bucket, a walking stick,
as a rhythm of bells
falls from the twilight.

Inside the barn I barely hear
their voices stir with hay smell
and shadow. A quiet follows,
the moment when the animals stop,
one by one at the wooden gate
for a hand they must lean against,
across the withers to the flank,
till they can step through
at the dark, each touch
closing behind them like a latch.

Tonight as spring lifts in the porch,
I watch how our lives
are gathered all by what we keep,
and suddenly I could run to them
and say it is beautiful
the soft lights pressing
through the redbud
and look how the Pleiades
shimmer over the hayfield
like a town we lived in
long ago, under the purple clouds.

Honey Locust

When the wind comes down the west hill,
the tall grass obeys, of one mind,
and you're alone there, suddenly astride the earth,
the eye going out upon the waves.
You try to walk, a hand in the tall hay,
wind warm in your ears, pushing your breath back
and you are empty as a blue sky
in the drunken joy of it.

At the top stand the ruins, fitted stones
fallen a century now in the swell and ice
of all its years. A nameplate on a rusted boiler,
a wagon wheel broken, its hub and spokes
scattered like a picture in the night sky.
Far below the creek runs low and clear
and a blue mist, like summer sleep
hangs in the thick wild maples.

In the wall is the jagged hole where a window once
looked out. The top half gone now, its stones lost,
and what was sight once is now half blind,
a cup of air drunk slowly by the years.
Alongside grows a honey locust.
From its trunk a single blossom,
pink the color of rose, opens, ringed
close by fists of purple thorns.

There is nothing here to weep for,
or lose your step. The waters run out
of the world no matter, and every joy
leaves the thinnest line of blood behind.
Or to pray for, or laugh, or think aloud.
But to go back down where she stands
by the flowers and billowed sheets,
he mends a door and their daughter
slaps the pond with a tiny stick, to go
down there plain and love them.

Beyond

My brother's ladder leans
to the smokehouse roof.
All morning he's been up there,
quiet in his work.

At last, when he calls to me,
"It feels like November now,"
the chilly wind seems to carry him off,
his shirt waving against the blue.

From the hill above the house
I look back to that world,
the paint shimmering red
in the level sun,
my brother's tiny movement
with his flag of a brush
swallowed by the sky.

From the hilltop, redbud and locust
rise into evening mist.
Above them stand the oaks,
still crimson, still full
and whispering.

Beyond, the clouds are blowing
westward and the holes
deep between them
where the stars fall through.

And beyond again, the other place
I would walk into, farther yet
till I would be wind and gone.
From a dark pane of glass,
a voice "Here I am.
Here I wait for you."

Stonework

Finally just a blue coat
moves in the twilight.
Nothing remains of those vanished labors
but a hammer spark, the hard rhythm
of stone on stone and the silence after
when thistles comb the wind.
Lost is the rising, falling hand,
a hat on the fence post blowing west,
smell of cold mud and anchored feet,
the gray hands cut and dried with lime.
All the bent-down sweet trouble
of the earth's arms we strain to be free of.

Tonight the hills lie white
up toward the ridge of cedars.
Cold fire pours from the sky.
Then the porch is lit; my brother
walks halfway toward the dark and calls.
Slowly the blue coat steps back
into human shape, trailing the night behind.
I stand near them, shadowed by the smokehouse door.
It is three years ago this month.
Some talk of work, hands measuring
a few small joys they hold like so many
invisible stars. My brother laughing
in his frail shirt as they tumble
from that minute they too cannot keep,
while greatness reels above their heads.

Bob and Alberta visited today.
They brought apples, a bushel of apples
spread out in the kitchen light.
Evening folds around them its blue-black dream.
All the meadow cold and sweet red
of that world I will never touch again.

I stay a while; we melt apart
and I am left to remember this way
because of love's measure, because night
slants down steep around a single
weary light and dust is everywhere.
Because death is a broken wheel.
Because the walls rise still unfinished
over snowy ground, worked with the dark
flawed stone and hammer of living memory.

Scything

There is silence in it,
the oiled stone drawn
down the crescent blade,
clean as frost,
ready for judgment.
The grass whispers
in its quiet sun,
over my shoulder
a handle of white ash bent
in the shape of a man.
No other sound all day
while my own breath leans
to the rhythm of gathering,
and the hayfield falling
sweetly down like the work
of the wind.

In a time when such a day
held both hope and need
and this, the new country,
called to them like the sky,
I stand awhile to work
within their strength
and see, through morning's
cool sweat, another face
beside me I've become
and other arms aching of wood
like mine. It is the real work
of the day, the shadows,
to bring the field home
with their belief, hay cradle
whispering, the arc of hay
swung overhead
dark and golden as thunder comes
and the tin roof hisses
in a vanished rain.

The Great Stone Wall of Camp Springs, Kentucky

In December I began, hauled stone
by truckloads to our border,
began a wall there. I was foolish enough then
to have a goal — to the Chinese chestnut tree
by Christmas, sliding on the apple rot
I carried from the cider press,
those cold days of rain.
And I was happy then.

I thought that was enough.
Then a little more, an afterthought,
on past the orchard, back down to the creek.
On the cupboard I kept a list
of reasons why I did it: to keep ideas out,
because it wasn't there,
win a dream trip to Cancún.

I think it was the morning
I hauled with Bob the first warm day
of the new year, it all changed.
We dug steps up the embankment
with a mattock, carried stones
or rolled them to the top,
heavier than ourselves. All morning,
all day till great piles stood
along the road.

The world passed us on the left.
A hand rose in the windshield
and we waved up, laughing,
the dark mud running down our arms,
our stomachs stained, finishing
the work of another century left undone.

All spring it was the same,
drank a little snakebite, up Four-Mile Creek,

Clarence Neltner's farm, across from the saloon,
Albert's land by his sister's house,
the abandoned road. Somewhere
I began to dream at night of stones,
the good fit, the good sound as they slide
and lock each other in. I felt the weight
in my sleep, woke wanting more.

To the north corner, behind the arborvitae,
across the island and up again
to the west hill where my brother planted grapes.
Eight hundred feet, the craziness of it,
a thing roughly like love that needs from you
life itself, or your death,
or some bargain in between
aching to go on, aching to stop.

I wanted to sweat.
I wanted to work
and beauty could wait till night,
when the moon burned stone shadows
on the ground. I wanted to carry the world home
knowing I would fail
and to know by that where life begins
and ends, and where home is.
Do all the things I shouldn't
and sleep at night.

Sycamore

I walked in sunlit cold
where the creek rippled
under first winter ice.
When my brother called
from near the road,
he was standing by a sycamore
he found, six feet or more across,
a tree so filled with time
these woods lay empty beside it.
Into two equal trunks
the tree divided, two great strengths,
their grains pressed into stone,
old as the nation.

Where they parted, a hole
had opened, so large we both
could stand inside, where leaves
gathered deep and living wood
closed around us. From above
a light came in and I saw beyond
the high limbs polished white
as driftwood in the sky.

One of the last to have stood
through years when this land
lay young to us
and our hatreds were as sweet
as what we loved, or were the same
and drove us there by a mighty hand.
Yet this tree grew,
the blood was washed,
sorrow carried westward on a gale.

And I listened, my hands
against its blackened walls,
to hear how the wind

16

would break it from the sky,
divide its heart a last time,
rain and earth claim all its past.
Yet today it stands
and *this* is life,
branches still witness to the sun
or flung to the stars,
a song of happiness as well.

The Necessary Stranger

Tonight, loss blows from the northeast
and snow with it.
I watch the cedars close, far up the valley,
their black coats to the wind.

Because we are still part of earth,
each winter brings to us again
the necessary stranger, the frozen ground.
Before them, we send a light out
from the window to hail the night,
an offering to the ancient cold.

But then we stand quiet on the winter field,
the furrows blown with snow,
and see the world return to us
other travelers like our own.
Seeds of light scatter high
in the brittle dark and the old legends
climb again in the east
with torches and their fate;
where a hand rises from the road
in passing and the dusk of human shape
wanders from a distant barn,
its lantern full of thought.

And if we let them in to share the fire
because the way is long and we are brief,
we find that they are one,
the journey and the meal,
the stranger here at supper and ourselves.

That together we make a blessing
of all these fragile lights, now most of all
in this darkest time of year.

Flathead Six

I

For thirty years it slept
in John Kramer's barn.
Men landed on the moon.
The dairy went broke.
We all grew up.
My brothers married.
For two hundred dollars it woke
and stretched into a world
that roared with daylight
and now sleeps in my brother's barn.
But on a Saturday one spring ago
we went for hay. The cat
jumped from the leather seat,
one tire threadbare,
the engine coughed and turned,
throttle out, riding the gas,
turned again, again.
My brother smiled over at me
"It's gonna start."

When it caught and roared awake,
in blue smoke the big frame
shuddered, a resurrection of parts,
a cool sweat broken on the hood.
"I saw a picture," he said to me,
"of trucks like this
on the mud steppes of Russia,
the Great Patriotic War."

II

Now Anna, who is two this month,
sits forward on his leg,
her hands apart as far
as she can reach. She looks ahead
and, laughing, looks back at him,
not certain yet which way to go.

For her, as each window of the day,
this too is still an act of faith.
Down Four-Mile Pike,
I see his face above hers
lean forward to the wheel
so slightly, far from the noise
in a quiet wind of the moment.
He was somewhere up ahead,
at the next bend, imagining,
or so I thought "I've read the plays
of Schiller, and all that might have been,
the city, those friends who slipped away
though we said never.
Now *this* is the road I'm on."

   III
The day was clear. Bottomland
gleamed with furrowed rain.
Four-Mile Creek wound high and muddy
beneath us, past bean fields
and sorghum and sycamores
brilliant in the blue.
With her there and her joy
how a cloud spreads
across the day, with highway
burning through the floorboards,
he looked as much a king as any
in his '46, or had what a king
sends armies for. That evening,
down the barn light a fine rain fell.
Everywhere people dreamed
as earth layered dark upon them.

That fall he hauled in apples
from the hill, pressed cider
on the lawn. The cat slept
on the flatbed in a bushel basket
filled with rags.

    IV
Praise to the man whose cistern
fills with rain, who hears
thunder as a birth of ground,
water its gift of heaven,
without complaint. Praise
the white horses in stillness
by the rusted gate,
beside their vanished plows,
the ground reclaimed in locust.
Praise things beyond their comforts.
Instead praise the ladders,
the bed made in the heart
because of them.

Wild Basil

When you sleep, how easily
you leave the world behind,
the cities yet to be,
the worried headlights
down the road. Tonight this hard rain
finally ended and clouds hurry west
like countries in a blue-black dusk
with stars in between.
A brown flood roars in the creek
under locust thicket
and wild grape.

But now you are awake.
I watch you ride up the hill
to the orchard, the tail
of Papa's blue coat soaring.
At the top you turn.
It is the first spring in your face,
its sharp wind, the new frogs
chirping, fireflies weaving
blankets in the dark.
How soon you will belong
to one another.

I stop and wave by the wild basil
at the window well where I work,
and from his arms you wave
back down to me, blessed
by a fire of things
untouched by knowing,
your smile the happiness
of rainwater on a cold morning,
overflowing its pail.

YOU WERE ONLY DREAM
AND I A GREAT ROOM
DREAMING YOU

Dragonfly

I see her cheekbones still flushed
with July, when we sat in the grove
of red oaks, that summer cicadas swirled
and cracked in the blue heat.
For hours we sketched the houses
along St. Gregory Street, shoulder to shoulder
climbing the hill, their slate roofs
gleaming, a tangle of wires foreshortened
on the sky. Maples drew the cool air in
and curtains waited, half aloft, each
with a face behind. All of it is memory,
so many years now, the high stone arch
with its colony of sparrows, streets
that echo down like ruins to the river,
each distance blurred in green and hot brick.

But here it is autumn, a time in the north
of holes torn in the sky, berries
and swept earth. The fabric of the season
no longer holds and the world gives way
to a mottled wind, the brittle rains.
Beside the garden fireweed unbraids into smoke.
From the ledge I lift the shell of a dragonfly,
its silver in my fingertips breaks
carefully in two. I think of her
as I let go and the cold seeds fly.
How once it was summer, the dragonfly
blue and full of lightning. Who is creator,
who scatters to the sky? Where is the oak now,
its flesh like furrowed stone
and the winged shade across her face?

But longing too must finally close
lest the dead own the living. All of them
now with glass hearts and their deeds

pressed into them like weathered tools
and us here with the weight of our eyes.
I walk back to the cabin light
with one of the names of God, Elohim,
protector who calmed the water,
said for her in her torchlit cave
and the dragonfly's brittle dust,
the word moving lightly before me
with the straw voice of the wind.

The Rose

I look for you
in the shadowed door
to come home below
trembling light
and black stone clouds
of an April night.
Spring is an ending too
and there I've gone for you
as one who lasted
the long dark and now
squints in the sun
unable to bear the new.
There I listen for you
where torn bark whispers
with warm light.
And you so nearly
step through its door
where I would follow
awaken and take your hand
on the first morning
of a thousand years,
and together run over
fields' driven green,
behold green redden
into flower, purple bind
the walls of the heart,
metal lace of dragonflies,
the blue cries, the silver
of the lovers' creation.
All doors with you,
through the skyward glass
of the eyes. But still
you are beyond and still
I seek you in a final drop
of sun on a wooden spoon,
a cobweb in a straight-backed chair,

$\frac{28}{O}$

    the iron roots of a yellow
    flower, a damp star,
    the unbearable rose
    of who you are.

Wooden Carving

From her face, wiped empty by a thumb,
her heart pours down the cloak
to gather her wooden child within.

When I touch her there,
against my fingers a first turning
of that world before the stars had fire.

Whoever took her eyes away
and left her in the world, alone,
the emptiness weeping ebony,

must have been freed as well.
It must have been the final day
on earth, when a black funnel roared

in a black sky, windows burst
and the waters all ran out,
when there was only time

to turn to her a last second
as if to carve again, to cut
the holes where the sun comes in.

Instead there was the artist's death,
death of the world, of what was seen,
what she now bears, the end,

the broken room, the rain-cold light, all
falling, falling in you as you watch,
a last shudder of love before night.

Starlight

Wind at my back,
the bonfire's shooting stars
die out as I lean against
this rake of a long day.

Night marks the seconds
winking across the birches
in this month of desire
all sap-green
on a March wind.

I want to go there,
to climb a stairway
I'd build to the weaver
beside the sea
who unwinds and winds
a thread of memory
on the brittle steel
needle of her heart.

The Heart

The wild grapevines
tangle empty in the winter sun.
Suddenly a redbird there
hangs his sudden fire down.
In the world sometimes
the smallest song reaches
to the ground so hard
it is ours already before
we turn to hear the snow
fall clean, the heart-red sound.
Winter berries make the coldest wine.
He was the meaning of his rhyme.

Spring

The soft spears of birch,
bitter still and cold.
Calving time, lantern and pain.
A green light waves in the north
each night, spilling finally
over the brightest stars.
All night in the house where I sleep,
the windows fill with bright water
and thrushes stream back
into their shadows with wild, solid joy.
An empty carriage waits at my door,
the desire of its invisible horses
nearly flesh in the south wind.

Summer

Each moment lover to the next,
the spun gown windblown,
the big stones of thunder falling warm.
Eternity and the hands make a cup for it.
Purple fireweed sings this way,
that way, berries tip their bowls
out on the ground. Even the cold
moths rise, their bright dust
drawn from an ancient clay.
When you must dream one day
come here, walk between the rain,
within your footsteps, the wild
strawberry sweet across the years.

Autumn

Beauty stands up one last time.
Frost binds the ground in chains
and the tendrils of stars grow longer
each night. Veil of wood smoke, a deep
crimson smell of harvest lost.
And if we are sad at nightfall
cold and red, it is not the leaves
that become our regret,
but how each face that lived in us
must fly. To know what must be
when black flames sprout
from the yellow tree, the heart,
touch and too soon are one.

Winter

Animals alone now keep the silence,
watching the world from within
their bones, wolf inside the wolf,
owl inside the owl, till just their
shadows hunt hard on snowy ground.
And for us too, that shape
we call spirit walks ahead
to measure us in this darkness.
One fragment of a leaf whistles
on its stem. How big night is,
how far the cities in the sky.
We light a fire; we long to be a fire;
we believe the angels sing.

Hannah

Tonight there is a south wind.
It is the end of May.
The green fields blacken
in the twilight into the colors
of their soil. Beyond,
on the great curve,
farm lights rise
in blue-white stars
that the earth pulls down
behind me as I go.
When you are older, I will tell you
of this night, when I drove
my truck across the prairie
and was alone and loved you
then as a real thing
though you were only dream
and I a great room dreaming you.
Someday you may tell your daughter
how I lifted you when you were small
till you brushed the sky and touched
the time in my face.
But such stories fall away
and then we sleep.
O my Hannah, all of it
was as I said, earth dark,
air sweet in my window
and that engine plowing
through the silence.
You came from there, flick of dream,
a handful of soil.
It was Ascension Thursday,
the Milky Way laughing,
the hush of Christ borne into heaven
and one red-winged blackbird
on the fence line, its mouth
open wide in wonder at the wind.

Tomorrow

There is an evening light as sweet as pain.
There is a pain we carted toward the sky.
There is a sky that crowns the earth with rain.
There is a rain to wash us when we die.

And we were these and everything, the hours
of rippled wind on rippled ponds of blue
you'd kneel to kiss in words more red than flowers
and I'd unjoin my ribs to let you through.

The glass of heaven shattered when you'd gone.
A tiny fist of petals shuts the rose
and stallion dark descends and gallops on
as cold rain whispers all the cold rain knows.

Each night my sleep that turns to you for home,
to touch your hair, wakes with your golden comb.

A CREATURE WHOSE
BRILLIANT EYES
YOU MISSED FOR ALL TIME

Sonnet for Woodstove

It melts the wax for candles. Both the cats
beneath it sleep inside their ancient dreams.
Our supper warms. The empty coats, the hats
imagine us. The fire within, it seems

are heaven's stars all gathered in one place,
a forge, a Bethlehem, a stellar heart.
If we are true, there grows on every face
an iron heat and window ice, both part

of the world no less. Make this a house of peace.
Make supper, grace. Make candles in the night.
Like smoke send threads of laughter up to crease
the sky. You know, as I, both dark and light

to see by. Stay awhile. Be here. Be fire,
a stove to burn the air up with desire.

Porch in Winter

Games of pool, blue twilight
river towns and the orange noise
of strangers through the screen door
that drew us there.

Of our victories and their thin escapes,
driving the high ridge midnight road
where the fog laughed
and fireflies joined the stars.

All talk is, in the end,
the talk of home. Twenty years
we have been friends.

From these chairs
we lean into our words tonight
like sails as the sun shifts,

board by board, behind the winter elm.
Then you lean back, unburdened, laughing
and I laugh too, in an hour forgetting.

It is what porches are for, to sit
awhile, watch before supper the cold
parabolas of swifts
and think of nothing more;

to talk, to listen for what is older
than ourselves. The heart. The rhythm
of the sea. Odysseus, who still longed
for home, though he was offered immortality.

Old Black Dodge

Morning was cold.
Even the cold half moon
crept in my coat
and sleep stung my face
in the blue and silver wind.
But we were gone by then,
down Saturday country roads
in my father's old black Dodge,
the privilege of that dark
before dawn in front of us.
Headlights jittered over
narrow miles, pushing
night aside just enough
for us to pass.
Through Milford at first light
where the glazed eyes
of houses stared so hard
I could feel their silence
on my face. At the high bridge
winter sycamores stretched
above the river rimmed with ice.
But we were warm,
climbing the long hill,
logging trucks ahead chained
with oak that we could never pass.
What we said is all lost now.
We were together on the road,
me on my Romex box, my father's
quiet cigarette as a cold sun rose.

All day he wired
the skeletons of houses,
villages without faces yet
or hearts, the wind unmapped
and free. I was his tool man,

ladder holder and built a fire
with scraps of wood
in each new hearth.
That was my job
and then we ate, his hands
red with cold, poured coffee,
hat pulled down, leaning
toward the fire,
looking at me. How clear
the day passed, like the sky.
Afternoon slipped by
and the Missouri Waltz
he always whistled in empty rooms
with years became the wind
itself those January days.

Then home, while evening
closed behind us.
I laid my head against the seat.
Those days I could still
let go into the grace
of things: the pure blue
nightfall that brushed
the windshield, shadows
climbing back in the barns
we passed, the shaded creek
wandering inside me.
Until my own twilight sleep
swayed in the shifting gears;
my father at the wheel,
quiet again as the country,
as we turned the road toward home.

The Burden

It was a roar of birches
that turned us from our work
as if a cave had opened
in the ground and its wind
hurled through the forest.
How low the bright trees bent
that first cold day of fall,
creaking in their skins.
But the leaves as they began to fly
and we in our old clothes
remained long past that year.
A few at first, but enough to keep us,
the blue sky of their joy
rising like a tower bell
for sons come home from war.
Then more were carried off
filling the wind, the wind
until the land lay empty
and a great wildfire autumn
blazed above us, crazy for heaven.
How close our silences stood that morning.
I felt my arms hang down,
the hammer in my fist grown heavy,
my feet spread out into the ground.
Higher again, nearly gone
till what seemed pure song at first
was equaled at last by the pull of earth.
And there they spun in those thin seconds,
now like human hearts,
as the prophet raised his horn.
Then all of us were one, to know
how happiness is both a sail
and a strength beneath us
that is harbor to our flight.
Snow that year fell early.

November circled overhead
and the moon struck the dark
like an empty kettle.
But because we stopped
once in our old clothes,
we found within our burden
the power to let our burden be
for an hour, a second
in the things of the world,
and were free.

All of Those Cigars

Thank you for those miles
you did not lead or follow me,
only the rain ahead of us
and a windy night,
collars up with a good cigar.
Where we went, we went
like stones thrown downward
from high above, both driven and drawn,
along and by the earth.

For hours we walked
into the lights of Anchorage.
Its tiny bowl of stars
touched the sky with the same
sad tales as ones drawn long ago:
of the hunt, of love,
of their beautiful defeat.

Today we look across those years,
each trail of smoke whirling with a memory,
one thought in front of us,
our laughter in the cold night air.
Below the roar of midnight planes,
through the rail yard,
cinder piles and silent lines
of freight, along the black
glimmering lake.
Past the whorehouses
with their dim blue lights.
I do not know what flickers
in their fingertips,
if life was once electric.

But tonight there is this road again
and we are walking in the rain.

And all of those cigars that went along
and did not come back
were long enough at least
so that we too did not return.
And what we thought we needed most,
all the longing for
that laid our faces bare,
we found in a final flick of ash,
a final star,
that we were already there.

The Lost

Lost beneath a lathe of constellations,
you dress the journey in knives and rags.
In the forest you kneel to touch
blood frozen in the snow
of a creature whose brilliant eyes
you know you missed for all time.
Then you look up from death,
a windless sail and the sky whispers
O in eternity what honey waits here!
Traveler, I would bring you home
to my wooden house and we could keep
silence together beside the stove
like another human heart.
And together be poor, the table set
with old stories lived again.
In your eyes I would watch
a hundred stars, the torches
of villagers who stumbled from their sleep.
How night climbs over them,
but they are singing and the song
is of a road and on the road
a child bends silently before the faces
of this bewildered world,
under the kingdom on his back.

Jason

I no longer remember
how my anger came,
or for what.
The cabin was small.
I loved his mother
but we were caught
in youth, unable
to free each other.
And he was five,
run off now
in the raspberry thickets
and sun of our lost year.
In an hour he returned
and came to me,
his arms around
the metal bowl like a
big globe of the world.
In the bottom
were berries, just four
or five, bright and careful.
I saw there how great
his struggle had been,
alone, and how
I left him in it.
I wish for him two things.
A faith to know
what's needed from the land,
and the faith
to bear it home,
now that he's a man.

Douglas

Up the road at his place, the harnesses
are hung inside and calendars
of all the years stacked on a nail.
One postcard, long ago, a friend
I never met "This year Katie will be five.
Time passes on." Sometimes we eat pizza
rolled out on the countertop,
cooked in the woodstove, drinking
port as night goes on.

But one night he took her,
Tasha, the dog who died last summer,
down in the woods, frozen in her blanket
and lit the pyre of brush built
in the fall, to let her shadow go.
No one ever knows what day
or where they parted. Once I asked.
He could not look at me.

Morning of the big snow he plowed my road.
I saw tractor lights in the starry dawn
and then him coming up the trail
for coffee, to dry and be warm.
I lit the lamp. We sat and talked
of winter. It is always this way.
Ten years and every year the same,
laughing at the cold, then quiet
a long time in our chairs, as if alone,
and never talk of love.

Bob Gunn

What more could I ask of your shadow now
than that gathering place you were
for us back then. For the janitors
and priests, for the beer man,
the maintenance crew playing the ponies
in the back each day at ten,
Jack my father's friend and his blind daughter,
Alex who lied about his age to fight for the czar,
Dennis who spent the war playing hearts.
As time makes them, they are silent now, as you.
The year-end party, all the profits spent,
the smell of beer on tile, after closing
in the back room by the safe. "Gentleness,"
you said, "and most of all respect,
now that's what women want."
I faced you in my chair, with my houses
yet to build, sorrow to take apart and fix,
seasons of rain and windows to hear the wind.
How could I understand?
Then you wished two things: for me,
children, out of sixty-two years of marriage,
to touch my own worth in that belief.
In your last letter, the wish for you,
and you said you did it, looked through
the giant telescope one night, above the trees
to the summer sky, at another traveler,
a wisp of methane ice, and came home
satisfied and slept,
having seen Halley's comet twice.

Woman with a Damaged Leg

As we left, she rose from her porch swing.
The screen door squealed and shut
and there she leaned, her weight half borne
by the wooden cane, and pointed to her flowers,
her white hair straight, her straight dress
white and plain. Hard on her cane and I saw
how a terrible wound had opened in her leg,
now ragged, begun to heal. A black dog
looked out, huge and silent, at her side.

"These are my marigolds," and she waved her hand
across them, "and here I planted zinnias,"
touching with her eyes atop each row.
"Will you come see them? Oh, I love my garden."
The rain-gray sky swept nightward
blue as a child's drawing and she, held
in the doorway, called us back, but we were gone,
"Yes they are beautiful," waving from the street.

Who is he there in uniform, along the grape arbor
in the wind, the boy without an arm?
Who are the girls in August, bare shoulders
leaned together, melon running down their arms?
The wedding, squinting in the sun,
the joy so fearsome in the morning air,
so for them death felt small and shrill
as a distant star. Tilted now, at rest,
along the bed, in mirrored shade
beside the unwound clock.

Who must not pass there, but we at last
through every room, by the pool black with leaves
and the broken fence wild in morning glories.
Even kings before their shattered armies,
the heartbroken, the immortal youth,
the child asleep. Even the saint blind
upon her stained sheet, whispering in thanks
the name of the Almighty.

OF THE HUNT, OF LOVE,
OF THEIR BEAUTIFUL DEFEAT

The Man Who Stood Still

And birds rose in the marketplace
    when the stones rang out,
And a carriage disappeared down the avenue
    when an empty pocket dreamed of riches,
And a woman flashed a curtain aside
    in her loneliness,
And a trumpet called to war
    all dark feet and hearts,
And parasols spread into butterflies
    as the cobblestones danced with rain,
And a ray of sun toiled
    through the graceful elms,
And a breeze drew back a thousand coats,
And all the hats smiled
    when the carnival rose at dawn,
And good and evil wrestled behind a dark window
    as the storm cloud hurried on.

In the photograph we watch again
how utterly they stepped into the past,
the carriage, the soaring coat,
each of their faces till just the ghosts
of buildings, like the dust
of half-remembered dreams, remained.

But the man who stood still while his shoes
were shined, who in his own time was late
to meet his lover, perhaps, or to a meal
still warm and he weary, thinking of tomorrow,
shows us now how fate is raw:
a mind in the high window with a camera,
one figure below, at ease, darkening in that lens,
how both waited long enough from perishing.

Then the man who stood still,
his face forever unknowable, would turn
at last and rush into time with them.

But for us, how he is chained there in the picture,
alone, as though we can feel him dazed,
lord of an empty kingdom
or a god when the stars go out.

Love Poem for Bluebells

Night settles over the ridges
where headlights rattle,
the road swallowed up
and a kestrel glides
at the willow tops, a silent
homebound spirit.

But I will stay with you
to wait as you wait
in the wind, though my own
eternity lies elsewhere.

We pass this way, our heads
bowed together in the black
thrust rock where I kneel
a moment beside you

to enclose a little time
from all the night
behind us and the one ahead.

How each face's downturned
lamp lets fall a drop
of light, cold as rain.
Now autumn in my hair

good-bye, you whose meaning
is but yourself and I step
back but you wait forever
in the quivering dark,

flames stirred by wind
as if in sorrow
for one who never died
and who was never born.

There Is Death I Said, Etc.

So I said to my friend
who came by as I stood
in the sun planing
lengths of fir for cabinets,
"There is another war out there.
I hear its heart on television,
where deeds become meals
of sorrow. It will not save them.
Now they wait on pallets
in the desert like medieval
woodcuts. Ribs enclose
their flesh as though death
has come out to cage them
from within, eyes alone
still great, candles whispering
in the black dawn,
by their brother's hand.
Then I see the boy
upright in the desert,
his garment and flesh alike,
sheets of hammered bronze
wrapped in a single
disappearance. Always
his eyes, growing
in the hot wind
and forge of the sun."
There was silence between us
then. Cruelty is our past
and what we leave,
as beauty is, a warm face
in the sun. From the ground
I took a fist of shavings
and held them up, blond
in the noonday light.

Like the reeds the wind
makes music of,
or the fallen curls
of a martyred son.
But that is not enough
when the straight light
comes down straight upon us.
And in that moment I find
I cannot look at you
although I must.

Sky, the Road, a Fire Between

Along the road in Kansas
I passed woman waiting in the cold.
The sun touched the prairie behind her;
land rolled beneath in green-black shadow.
An evening star hung in twilight
from the barn. For that second, I saw
her coat, the white breath rising
and her eyes looking off, upward
to where nothing is but the sky's
blue stone heart.

Five hundred miles, all night
I thought of her, how between
one face and heaven stretched
a thin glass column to draw
her longing up. For me it is three years
and I am going back to the rain
at Christmas and Scorpio blowing
in the oaks again, where my own
mysteries crease my face and clouds
slip in the moonlight, as in youth.

But here sleep burns my eyes
at first light, more empty road ahead.
Then a great flock of starlings
rush above me, west to east,
all of one heart. Where are you going?
says the sky. There can be peace
without understanding, the moment
a thousand wings darken the sun
shaken from the wheat field
one morning at the end of time.

Sonnet for Unknown Child

Tonight the leaves put on their skin of sleep.
Tonight the wooden hands reach into stars.
Regulus, frost in his shaggy crown, keeps
whispering in the east. A face looks far

off toward the midnight whistle of a train
crossing that land we both have traveled through.
Come closer now to hear its great cold chain
struggle at the night. In moonlight's first blue

shadowfall, I'll drink to winter light
that we be shepherds as they were long ago,
who traveled far, with no homeland in sight.
One star, a voice, dark road and nothing more,

to find it was a child they came to bless.
The cave was cold. Upon their faces, wilderness.

Sea of Storms

All the nights I spent
cold at the telescope
while the neighbors slept,
in one moment by chance
I see them, one line of geese
flying west, in the mirrors
upside down, over the Sea of Storms.
So high, those waters
could be their home.
I look away and back again
till they are past
out in the frozen dark,
the quarter moon waving
as the earth cools.

There is a place I often drew
as a child, where the trees at sunset
hovered black like wooden fire
and in the thicket underneath
a path was cut – for a voyager
to rest as I think now.
In its center I placed
a tiny flame, to cup in both hands.
It was to hold in my coat tonight,
for I saw how cold and straight
was their flight and I
was mapless and afraid,
standing in the wind
as a young man
for the last time in my life.

Antonín Bečvár's Atlas

Come night again,
that sweet alone
with this book of the sky
open on a stool.
In flashlight, the clear
grid of the mind
is placed and turned
upon the chaos
only to look up again,
beyond order, to the blue
quills of the stars

where others may look back
with the same unanswered eyes.
If we raised our hands
together, no fuel
our thoughts could burn
would bear that light,
quivering, in time
before we are dust.

Morning comes finally
over the dew
like lovers' sheets
and I wake to this map
of the day so easily
given, the spell broken.

Yet sewn inside her cloak
on the dark side
of the world, I hear
the galaxies of Cassiopeia
whirl like blooms of
wildflowers on a windy night.

Boxcar

On the prairie of Saskatchewan
a single boxcar stands
on rusted siderails plunging
through lost rusted grain.
Both side doors now stand open
to a hundred miles of wheat beyond,
the shadows long ago drained
in the ground. Easily the wind comes,
wheel after wheel the hours turn,
rolling out and into history.
The men who rode here, the rags
of their eyes, blow now
in the great steel window.
Their pockets still dream
with fists of dust in them,
their money spent on squares
of the sky. Far-off lightning pours
under the prairie moon.
Through those doors purple night
gathers, where a black rain funnel
draws to its fierce whirling heart
those lost ones, the steel machinery
of their hope, a vein of light
blinding in the marrow drawn,
hurricane to the sky, fires
of all that was in them
to say they were for something,
to say it is not complete,
that armies of the angels
still collide above, swords drawn
in passion for our souls.

Dinner with Jack Palance

In a restaurant like an English inn,
the antiques imported, screwed to the walls
and everywhere overhead a feel of torches
flickering. Well, that's the place I went
one night when Jack came in, and his wife.
He took her coat, sitting below a portrait
of the duke and his hounds. Of course I joined them.
Our dinner was cordial, and later we met
at the river, flooded and wild and pulled our boats
to shore. Then we walked the high bridge
lined with tiny shops while water raced thick
beneath us like a channel of molten steel.
Though we did a few strange things together,
I liked his movies; I liked his style.

Unlike one other night when the woman
at the reservoir looked into me. We never spoke.
We were in love. At last I felt the daylight
come and pull me from behind, to a doorway
where the brightness roared like a great machine
big as an ocean drawn and loosed across the land,
where I had to go so I could live and she knew
it was the end. And so she crumbled,
her face, her black eyes scattered.
But these are only the gears of death,
how a thing works, when the heart flickers out
and a thread is tied to us unwinding from that place,
however far we walk. Yet she was something more.
For she saw her death approach, stunned
with its night, and I watched her fill with a terror
of the innocent trapped inside a place
she wandered to and now must share its fate.
All the things she knew, the horror, love,
forgiveness in those broken eyes and letting go
in a wash of dust, none of it was mine. How I sat
that morning in the sun and thought of her
and thought of what the night had done.

Around the worlds we make lies a greater dark
we cannot know, where creatures may come
and love us, a place where I may find myself one day,
delirious, while the stonework of the sky falls in.
But that is the price of a world.

I don't want to go there for a long time now.
Though dinner again with Jack Palance would be fine,
and his lovely wife with the hairdo, Jack
with the cigar and me thinking how evil he was
in all those movies, but that of course was an act,
he isn't evil at all and the dinner was splendid,
candles, a table for three, you know,
nothing fancy, just dinner and polite farewells.

The Doorway

There is the moment of the day
in early June, when yellow light
falls on the equisetum and the ground
breaks out so luminous, so green,
could winter ever fall atop
such beauty and lie so foreign,
so deep? I watch from my doorway
how the light moves off, grows pale
finally, the way a face falls
out of memory. Behind me,
through the door are all the things
I have, part of the world grown
used to me. And beyond at the twilight
woods, what will gather me
tomorrow. But now I let go
in the gentle, given night, unearned,
and settle in the door
(while the unmoving part of me
still turns to you to speak love
always). But soon we must be still.
For a rain begins to fall, so fine
that the woods fill up
with silver light
but make no sound.

ABOUT THE AUTHOR

Joseph A. Enzweiler was raised in Cincinnati, Ohio and was educated at Xavier University and the University of Alaska. Magazines and periodicals in which his poems have appeared include the *Spoon River Quarterly*, *Journal of Northern Kentucky Studies*, and *SouWester*. His first book, *Home Country*, was published by Fireweed Press. He lives in Fairbanks, Alaska.

This book was designed by Will Powers. It is set in Perpetua type with Klang titling by Stanton Publication Services and manufactured by Quebecor/Fairfield on acid-free paper.